JINX

Abigail Parry spent seven years as a toymaker before completing her doctoral thesis on wordplay. Her poems have been set to music, translated into Spanish and Japanese, broadcast on BBC and RTÉ Radio, and widely published in journals and anthologies. She has won a number of prizes and awards for her work, including the Ballymaloe Prize, the Troubadour Prize, and an Eric Gregory Award. Her first collection, *Jinx*, was published by Bloodaxe in 2018.

ABIGAIL PARRY

JINX

BLOODAXE BOOKS

Copyright © Abigail Parry 2018

ISBN: 978 1 78037 234 1

First published 2018 by
Bloodaxe Books Ltd,
Eastburn,
South Park,
Hexham,
Northumberland NE46 1BS.

www.bloodaxebooks.com
For further information about Bloodaxe titles
please visit our website or write to
the above address for a catalogue.

Supported using public funding by
**ARTS COUNCIL
ENGLAND**

LEGAL NOTICE

All rights reserved. No part of this book may be
reproduced, stored in a retrieval system, or
transmitted in any form, or by any means, electronic,
mechanical, photocopying, recording or otherwise,
without prior written permission from Bloodaxe Books Ltd.

Requests to publish work from this book
must be sent to Bloodaxe Books Ltd.

Abigail Parry has asserted her right under
Section 77 of the Copyright, Designs and Patents Act 1988
to be identified as the author of this work.

Printed in Great Britain by Bell & Bain Limited, Glasgow, Scotland, on
acid-free paper sourced from mills with FSC chain of custody certification.

The *iynx* was understood to work by emitting a sound that was seductive and persuasive but that also – like so many seductive and persuasive sounds – was possibly deceptive, spelling ruin for its listener [...] Not only does Jason's use of the *iynx*, like all improper means of persuasion, bring grief to its victim, it also brings grief to Jason himself eventually.

SARAH ILES JOHNSTON,
The Song of the Iynx

ACKNOWLEDGEMENTS

Thanks are due to the editors of the following publications in which some of these poems first appeared: *All My Important Nothings* (smith|doorstop, 2015), *Aquanauts* (Sidekick Books, 2017), *Asterism* (Laudanum, 2016), *Birdbook II* (Sidekick Books, 2012), *Falling Out of the Sky* (The Emma Press, 2015), *The Asahi Shimbun, The Compass, The Live Canon Anthology* (Live Canon, 2015), *The London Review of Books, Magma, The Moth, Naso Was My Tutor* (The Emma Press, 2014), *Observations/Transformations* (The Lawrence Sterne Trust, 2015), *Oxford Poetry, Poems in Which, Poetry London, The Rialto, The Spokesman* and *Wild Court.*

'Arterial' won the 2016 Ballymaloe Prize, 'Pasodoble with Lizards' won the 2016 Troubadour Prize, and 'Key' won the 2016 Free Verse Competition. 'Phantom' was commissioned for broadcast on the BBC Radio 3 series *Southbank Poets*, and 'Into' was installed on Guernsey bus routes for the 2017 *Poems on the Buses* exhibition.

I am grateful to the Society of Authors, the Hawthornden Trust and Goldsmiths' College for their support and encouragement. My love and gratitude to the great many individuals who have given me their time, enthusiasm and kindness, and in particular to Maura Dooley, Sarah Barnsley, Christopher Reid, Jo Shapcott, Bernard O'Donoghue, Neil Astley and Jon Stone.

CONTENTS

Emma, you're a gamer

Seldom, very seldom, does complete truth belong to any human disclosure.

Emma, you're a gamer. Backgammon, anagrams,
the matches and the banter.
                You're a natural. Serve and volley
back and forth in argument – the provocation, the resolve,
those little zigzags of embarrassment –
            one hundred different ways of being in love.

Emma, you're a dreamer. You're a strategist, a schemer –
the metagame of manners,
          all those formal misdemeanours,
the compliments, charades.
              Emma, you're a charmer.
You're a looper and a reeler. The surliest grammarian
would melt to see you dance.
             Emma, you're a gamer.
Who knows better than the dealer
the hazards and the chances, the advantage of a match,
the ricrac interlock of suit and fortune?

Oh Emma, it's a screamer. All the riddles, the enigmas –
the courtship in a sonnet,
          the conundrums on the hill.
Yes he's frank, but is he candid? Someone blundered,
someone's bluffing,
          and someone's slipped a joker in the pack.
The letters on the table rearranged to name your error –
Emma, you're a goner, don't you know you've met your match?

Emma, that's *amore*. So it goes, same old story –
the word you didn't know,
          the trick you had to miss.
The hint that every night has sat and stared you in the face
while you punted little sallies to and fro.
          Give it up now, little ego,
there's a prize for second place,
and Emma, you're an amateur, you're up against a pro.

Hare

You dreamed the field was a tin grid,
latticed with running hares, March-mad and stargazy,
their quick jolts the firing of neurons.

At other times you meet him alone:
that long face, the dowsy parting at the mouth,
a suggestion of teeth; lecherous, repulsive, somehow
irresistible. *Witch*.

And he was there in pinstripes,
haunches drawn out on their pivot,
leaning over your shoulder at the wedding party,
those fine ears folded smooth down his back,
complacent. Smug. Buck-sure.
His yellow eye met yours, knowing
you could do nothing. You thought

I'll have you, you suave bastard.

Find him in a field. He's gone
in one swift arterial pump.
                        Oh, he is a tease...

        He is the sidelong, sidling
and askance,
        so learn to see as Hare sees,
        learn his steps,
accept his invitation up to dance –
he'll stay that spring-heeled jolt if you keep time.
Walk in rings around him. Do not spare
        one glance towards the centre or he'll bolt.
See how a pattern's there, a coiled line –
        tighten up the circles, and each whorl
will shave a sickle off the verticil.
        Pare away the moons. His labyrinth's
a unicursal round: with just one end,

and just one track. He'll be waiting,
slant-eyed jack, and prince
  of tricks. Your part is fixed:

  a virgin going down,
  a widow coming back.

The Lemures

Something is digging the stuffing from the old red plush
of the seat behind you in the darkened theatre.
And later, with the rain falling not-quite-right
in the headlights, and the odd half-glimpsed zigzag,
and the cat's eyes coming unstuck, that soft tug-
tugging at your collar grows insistent: they are still here.

Still here, with their quick fingers and luminous eyes,
their spook faces, their fingers hooked like questions.
You meet them half way, know them from halfway places:
the empty A-road, the mezzanine, the bent
reflection in the lift doors before they purr
open again on the things you know: phones ringing, people.

They are a nuisance. They have so many questions
and no respect for the living. They prod and pinch,
they stare. They paw at the glass between what is yours
and what is theirs. Do not feed them – they will always
want more. They will steal from you. Pickpockets,
rifling the snug pouches at the back of the mind,

and that one narrow finger grubbing, rat-a-tat,
for your soft spot. They never stop. They belong to you
and they will wait for you – in the borders of the wet garden,
the silence behind the beech hedge. They hoard rubber balls
and the past and all your lost things, and always want to know
when you're coming back, when you're coming back, when.

J♥

He that must use them, take this rule from mee,
Still trust a knave no further than you see.

SAMUEL ROWLANDS, *The Four Knaves*

Sworn   bachelor
and dandy, man-
about-the-town.
Snook-cocker, fancy-
man, catch-him-if-you-can   man.
  Peacock-suited, booted, pretty-boy,
 fop. Too nimble for the altar, too dashing
for the chop.   One eye's for the ladies
the other's on the crown   Back-
doorer,   in-and-outer,   turn around,
he's gone.   Trickster, twister, wild-card,   liar
Now he's in a Landau   Now a Black Maria.
Rich man,   Poor man,   Ragged man,   Prince,
Steerpike, climber   Give the man an inch!
  Springheel, charmer, haven't-caught-him-yet.
    Hard-to-get, hopeless case, straight-up
    bad   bet. Two-face, double-crosser,
                        table-talker,   crook.
                    Player, faker, heart-
                    breaker,   ladies'
                    man, I'm hooked.

13

The Man Who

Wow boy you've got some nerve –
bitten down,   a sliver of live line,
stuttering filament,   blown,
wired up all wrong, strung out
and going like a striplight, *too
thin, I tell you, you're too thin!*
A shock   a finger-in-a-socket,
blue, electric blue   and fine,
fine like cocaine, fine like flickknives,
scissored-out, snuck out the back of the
catwalk, fine like nail files,
                        first live birth
of the space age,   dead in the wreckage
but always climbing out, always stepping
through a door
                in the new, new
white-hot new,
cut in acrylics, crystalline,
one hundred thousand miles
of chrome and foil,
     or wicked in pinstripes, drainpipes,
slick, tooled up
                        but kid,
what happens when the mask sticks?
What happens when the ice stays stuck?
Leaving you
hollowed out like a flute, like a pinion sunk
in the heart of boy like you –
          then you've got to burn out –
down to the fingers, down to the quick,
to the quick quick heart of a white-hot
boy like you
who could strut and preen, burn up
                and then roll over

14

who stitches catsuits from his ogres,
on first-name terms with all the scary monsters –
SCUM   PERVERT   WEIRDO   FREAK
nothing sticks to you,
                  but fuck, weren't you
everything we feared, and all we wanted?

The Knife Game

Thumb

A narrow time: one summer long,
if that. Old enough to know

that we're no longer children, though
we've not yet grown into

the high, clean mountain air
of common sense, where games like this

would make us wince.
There are no rules as such. You spread your hand

and push the fingers wide as fingers go.
The blade stands by your thumb. You start off slow.

Index

The kitchen winces taut. There's nothing
but the pert
tut tut of steel in wood.

The trick's to start off slow,
precise, telic. Plot
each secant line and then return it home.

Middle

The trick's to keep it low –
skimming knuckle skin, out
and in, and in
     and out,
         Again.
  Again.
A wicked tat, a quickening refrain,
  A picked-up stitch, a knitting machine,
     A pat-a-cake,
A tic-tac-toe
     that zeroes
   on an
     O

Ring

The trick is not to yelp.
A wince is fine, a grit, and you can let

your open mouth bite on that silent O.

But O – that sharp, expected
quick surprise –

and O – our rusty prints, the sticky
salt-and-iron taste of yours and mine.

Little

And the next day, and the next,
that queasy ache –

split nail, split skin,
slit cuticle, two dozen little nicks.

I eat my meals in forkfuls. My left hand –
inert, potato-eyed – lies in my lap.

But if I wince it to a fist, it's there –
the drub of blood at every scabbing point.

Two dozen hidden doors. Two dozen mouths.
They open on a secret: mine and yours.

Knife

Unluckiest of gifts, it severs ties
between giver and receiver. By September

you're getting served in bars,
and I've been packed off to a different school.

A giddy vertex, that – the point
we set an angle on divergent lives.

Already, you know how to make a boy
do anything you want a boy to do. Already, I

know better than to play with girls like you.

The Wolf Man

> Of course I believe that *The Wolf Man* is the best of my horror films –
> because he is *mine*.
>
>   LON CHANEY JR.

You can't know how it feels –
to have the blood

bark backwards through the heart,
and every nerve snap shut.

That's how it was, each time
I saw that name, my father's name, mine

but not mine.
              The man himself

played twenty roles a week, could lose
both legs and break his back by close of day.

The Miracle Man, The Hunchback, The Unknown,
the man with a thousand faces, every one

his own. The work of a craftsman.
I watched him grind the lenses,

strap himself in homemade trusses,
bind his limbs, bend over backwards

till his back was broke for good, spine buckled,
his eyes spent. Everyone had a piece:

the studio took his arms, his legs,
his face a thousand times. The talkies

killed the pantomime, but even his voice
was acrobat – till that went too.

Then only his name was left
                              – and I took that.

The day they repossessed the car –
furniture gone already, business sunk.

Only his name was left. I couldn't hock it,
so I wore it. It swallowed me in one gulp.

Those years were hungry years, scavenging
bits and scraps, giving away a good name

for third-billings and extras,
stunt work, cowboys, thrillers.

And Christ, the man's shadow! Sure,
it opened doors, but then each night

it grew long and tall, and came capering
up behind me, like the hard–

faced harbourmaster, waving *go back go back*.
Go back to what? The country starved.

I grew thin behind that name, impalpable.
I grew cold behind that name, insatiable.

A thickset ghost with a heavy burden,
uncertain, lumbering. A ghoul. That is,

till I found the Wolf.
                              Makeup took the credit,

but the Wolf was mine,
I found him in me. Only I knew the Wolf,

how I'd nursed him in the stony, coldest
part of myself, chewing on nothings,

mouthfuls of ash and a brain of diamonds,
a bellyful of ice and a brain in ribbons.

A man lost in the mazes of his own mind –
But when I walked, I felt the sprung

piston of haunch and shank, a tread too
firm to be faked. And when I opened my mouth,

I spoke from far off,
a lean and craggy country,

and behind it piped the high
grave falsetto of the Wolf. And oh, oh,

When the Autumn moon is bright...
Those hours were mine. *Mine.*

A word to follow home.
A word to bite down on.

The Oracle

I

You love the word long before you learn
its stingy meaning.
Dry, and hollowed out

like snailshell, it has the choral click
of mussels jostled in a wicker pot;
so you put it where it fits —

at six years old,
your oracle is a sparrowskull.
Wafer-dry, its thin dome hugging

a small, snug dark.

II

Sunday, 12 p.m. Off go the gloves like lizardskin
and with them goes the slew of graven
images, genuflections and Corinthians.

The words don't let you in. Their fine scaffold
of tracery and transept, scrolled and elegant,
obdures in the ecclesiastical chill

and keeps its distance. *In principio erat verbum* —
that part you understand, though understanding
is a plodding, humdrum thing, not like the quick fix

of a good incantation: its whiplash logic.

III

You keep another altar. In the briar thicket,
the rhododendron dark, the wrought work
of praxic fern. In the tabernacle quiet

of a Sunday afternoon, rooting
for the hidden brickwork and the rusting grille.
The oracle, your oracle, is within.

Just look: the bony pate, the terse-set beak,
the vaulted sockets and their printed frown;
it is a dry professor, coddling

a lunatic wit in that eggshell brainpan.

IV

It speaks a wasp-language, mouthed in sawdust corners,
confessional. Heathen nonsense of taps and clicks,
struts and echoes, and a huge, surging whisper of the dark

music in things: a choral clamour
of organ reverberations. And you're a lost cause –
you take many gods,

rattle necklaces and call yourself *pagan*
because that word is a peg staked
in the thick turf of private hallowed ground

that Flyaway Paul and Comeback Peter,
Matthew, Mark, and all their Latin cannot budge.

The fuss you made about your wedding veil

When thin enough, it's called *illusion*
which will always mean to me
Claude Rains, in 1933,
hurling his nose at the gathered crowd.
The villagers look on dumbly (as do I
from several decades down the line
one rainy Sunday afternoon).
The landlady, screwed up into her bun,
shrieks her famous shriek. Off come the goggles,
off, in furious rounds,
the wound-round bandage covering no wounds,
no face at all. The bobby's first to speak.
Look, he says.
He's all eaten away. A horrid phrase
and one I never could dislodge –
not when the credits rolled, or when I learned
about mattes and velvet screens, and Rains
fussing, claustrophobic in his suit.

Afraid of what? Perhaps to be the first
to feel himself winked out
before the eyes of the gathered crowd, and by
the ruthless magic of a spectacular age.
How seamless it all seems –
how easily one might just
fade to black
        or slip between
twelve different shades of white,
and edged or plain, and tulle or net,
bandeau, birdcage, juliet –
yes. I think I'd make a fuss as well.

Goat

Don't fall for it – the sidelong look, that punted puck
of a pupil – Goat wants nothing more

than to slip a cleated mitt beneath a fuss of skirts,
raise merry hell.
                    Button up. Keep very still.

Don't think about that knock-kneed hopscotch,
dapper, quickstepped, keen. The long, tall grin.

Goat means to take your shoulder as a bit
between his teeth, skip in and out like nifty ribbonwork.

Call him Stickpin. Call him *Sheershank*.
Don't call to him at all –   *But oh, my girl, you will.*

Call it fancy. Call it whim.
Call it a door opening on the slant stair

to the room you didn't know was there,
                    though you've lived here all your life –

                    And come down with the dawn.
Now you've been gone too long –

the dance was over weeks ago, your guests
have all gone home.
                    Now you're shoeless, skint

and swindled. Now the daybreak wants to know.
Now the piper's piping up beyond the gate –   *too late, my girl, too late.*

You Know Who

Some actors fear if they play Sherlock Holmes for a very long run the character will steal their soul, leave no corner for the original inhabitant.

JEREMY BRETT

See how it glints and sparkles! Every good stone
is a nucleus of crime, every facet a bloody deed.

Oh yes, the hither-thither razor zips from crown
to culet! Quite so. But what may be said of the bullet,

which has struck the windowframe, just here?
What of the extra glass, and the shorn-off fire iron?

The facts, now, just the facts. We have a body,
and a murderer. Who, then, was our third drinker?

Who is our guest, who smokes without a holder,
who paces as he waits, and rubs his hands together?

Whose is the greatcoat, whose the bloody print
on the newel post? Whose the multi-tool knife

that nicked the bellrope? Who is this black streak,
this jackal, this jewel thief? And who, who is it

who coughs in the attic room? Let us fall back
on the old axiom. But tell me, my dear Watson,

who is this lean thing in the sanatorium,
with the door fastened from the inner side?

Tell me the truth now. Do you not think it
a most singular and whimsical conundrum?

†

Bailiff, or bouncer. Handiwork of a cutthroat.
Killjoy to your better half's starburst. Skip-beat
and spikenard. Rum goings-on in the upset messroom.
Last ditch attempt in the gone-wrong exorcism.

Skulldugger, scoundrel. Sole suspect in the scandal,
tyrannical empress, the needle that trembles
and points to the necklace. Lone cypress
in the boneyard. Skinny bloke fingering his timepiece.

Brilliant flourish of textual cross-stitch. Spit or dart
or tip of a javelin. Splint in the margin, arête
in the plainsong. Exit of choice for the suicide-king.
Painstaking, ruthless – the hairline dividing

the clerk, the assassin. Enviable cousin
of furious cross-hatch. Every draft binned
because you were the subtext. Black mark of the culprit.
Tell-tale heart, and the compass that finds it.

Girl to Snake

We're not supposed to parley, Ropey Joe.
I'm meant to close my eyes and shut the door.
But you're a slender fellow, Ropey Joe,
                    thin enough
to slip beneath the door and spill your wicked do-si-do
            in curlicues and hoops across the floor.
I'll be here. And I'm all ears –
there are things I want to know.

> *Oh tell me tell me tell me*
> *about absinthe and yahtzee,*
> *and sugarskulls and ginger, and dynamite and hearsay,*
> *and all the girls and boys who lost their way*
> *and the places in the woods we're not to go*
> *and all the games we're not allowed to play –*
> *there are so many things to know.*

My mother's got the supper on the go.
My father will be sagging in his chair.
But you're a speedy fellow, Ropey Joe,
                    quick enough
to slide behind his back, a wicked line of dominoes
            zipping through the hall and up the stairs.
Come on, pal. I'm ready now –
there are things I want to know.

> *Oh tell me tell me tell me*
> *about lightning and furies*
> *and ligatures and diamonds, and zipwires and gooseberries*
> *and all the girls and boys who went astray*
> *and all the ones who never got to go*
> *and all the words we're not supposed to say –*
> *there are so many things to know.*

They told me you were trouble, Ropey Joe.
You've always got to tip the applecart.
But you're a subtle fellow, Ropey Joe,
                    suave enough
to worm your way inside and pin your wicked mistletoe
          above the crooked lintel to my heart.
Come on then, shimmy in –
there are things I want to know.

> *Oh tell me tell me tell me*
> *about hellhounds and rubies*
> *and pretty boys and bad girls, and runaways and lost boys*
> *and all the things that made my mother cry*
> *and all the things he said to make her stay*
> *and all the things we're not allowed to say –*
> *there are so many things to know.*

俳諧の連蛾

Common White Wave

Barely there –
the white way through the lilacs.
Last year's confetti.

Peppered moth

Headstocks on the skyline –
jerking polygraph.
Little turncoat.

Ringlet

Hush hush of haircloth,
busk, fourchette; blind eyelet
and the eye that sees it.

Six spot burnet

Old bloodspot moon
and his silk suit: the dark
jester in full slap.

Brown silver-line

Lips part like that –
the velveteen head, bursting,
then fullblown, ruinous.

Death's-head hawk-moth

The dance in full swing
and that slender fellow there,
cracking his knuckles.

Monarch

The terrace at midnight:
white jasmine, and that room
lit from within.

Reedling

I

More bauble than bird, a merry bobbin,
a balled-up sock. One button chuckling among many.
Strawberry-plump, and pipped

with achene eyes: your first inkling
of something awry. They seem
glued on, the stiff glass of waxworks.

Drag the memory banks. You can think of them
buffed in bronze, iced in strawberry pink,
paperweight-solid, or chumming it with finches

in your grandmother's lacquer-black cabinet, but never
as moving components. And now
– though you have never noticed them before –

they are everywhere – nested
among satsumas and buff paper, or cupped
where an apple should be, an egg, a breast.

They peep from tea sets, hunker
in ice-cream scoops, optics.
One nubbed bit plugs

another's socket – fills
the open mouth of an opened question.
That's how the puzzle fits.

II

We are a scattered thing – imagine a fibrous net
globe-wide, and stuffed with reedlings!
This is a thatch of ropey cells, busy.

A burst pillow. A smashed snowstorm.
The mind fizzes with circuitry. When it leaks,
what flies out? We are thinking

a cracked pot, steam wheedling from it
in flighty puffets. The mind, they say, is
whatever it is thinking. Now we are thinking

that our eyes are not hard seeds, but
liquid fossils, pinholes on prehistory.
We are awesome saurines, rolled into fat-balls. We are

so very many, maddeningly so,
and lodged like bulbs. The mind
is filled with pockets: things root.

Don't look too long. Our call
is the soft, futile ping of a giving hinge.
The mind is filled with pockets,

and things come home to roost.
Our rebus spells something elusive, nagging,
known. Forgotten again.

Good Morning, Captain

The Captain counts destroyers –
Dauntless, Diamond, Decoy, Dragon,
corrals them one by one into his dock.
And when he's done destroyers, he starts on submarines –
Voracious, Venture, Vanguard, Vulpine, Vox.

And when the Captain dreams,
he dreams of all the things he's seen –
the fire on the glacier, explosions in the sea.
The Captain's been a hero. The Captain's done it all.
The Captain's got a lot of glitzy pins.

And when the Captain dreams,
the girls are wearing slinky things –
Emma, Lucy, Sarah, Charlotte, Claire.
The Captain's had his sweethearts. The Captain's seen it all.
The Captain's been the cat who got the cream.

And when the Captain dreams,
he dredges nightmares from the sea –
the slurpers and the suckers, the scuppered and the sunk.
They come with open mouths. They tick upon the hull.
They walk on crabby stilts and *whisper* things.

And when the Captain wakes,
he wonders why it's ten o'clock,
and who put pastel flowers up the walls.
Good Morning, says the bedspread. *Good morning*, says his life,
the slipknot sliding shut around his neck.

The Captain counts his children
from the photos in the albums,
thinks a thought, then chases it away.
And just on the horizon, tacking fast, the wind behind her,
that little speck that's closer every day.

Black Lagoon

Even I, Lucas, have heard the legend of a man-fish.

But what did they tell you, Lucas?
Out of the murk and mystery –

was I all pleats and webbing, spats and pipes,
my wet heart thrashing for *lovely Julia Adams*?

I live here all alone. The water looks
like screens look after everyone's gone home.

Don't you know me, Lucas? Don't you recognise
this place? That flarestick *I* means nothing here,

your beacon name's a dud. Who's this
who walks the bank? And who could say

what backlit tricks the mirror plays
with lights and cameras muffled for the night?

The Amazon chugs turpid gold and greens
through California's glitz – *smiles, tinsel,*

yesses, fizz – the extras stick their tacky skin
to plastic slats of loungers. Oh Julie, Rita, Kay –

each night, in phosphorene, you've loved the lot –
hot, pliant, all lit up like slot machines.

Lucas, when they named you, did they say
what draglines ran below? What languid things

resisted in the current? Oh Lucas, did they say
that each man has his double in the dark?

And when I climbed aboard, what else
was struggling, upwards, gagging on the light?

The Stone Girls

I *Rodin: Danaid*

Not the unfinished face, the flush of useless hair,
but the length of her: how she stretches

belief almost to breaking, angled, cocked
on that immovable pelvis, the stern

truss of muscle between the shoulders,
yanked and locked. How absolute

the back is in its syntax. How fitted to the task
of indexing, and figuring, despair.

II *Ives: Undine*

Feels
heavier, and is
heavier. Feels

the downward suck
planting each foot, the tug

of hook in lip, is
jackknifed upright. Knows

that underjaw itch, the straining
on thin air. Forgets

the grave electric roar
of salt on shale, the bottle-blue dark. Remembers

nothing. Dies
through the mouth, and feels
nothing.

III *Saint-Gaudens: Caryatids*

Give us a smile,   Chin up, might
Love.   never happen.

      Aw, c'mon,

          don't
be like that   Frigid bitch

boy, you're gonna   *carry that weight*
carry that weight   *a long time.*

Milagros

Sump hearts, sluicing.
Pyx hearts, with one tinfoil coin skittering.
Porcelain hearts scaled in lime.
Lamprey hearts, sucking on dead ones.
Brinkman hearts stretched on the racks of dead stars.
Icarus hearts fired to clinkers.
Cabinet hearts chocked with trinkets.
Supple hearts trained with twine.

      Strung like piñatas
      or propped like imperial eggs:

Minnow hearts routed. Hearts frittered to confetti.
Hearts smeared in porpoise oil, dropped in the Drink.
Marionette hearts jangling a waltz
in a last chance last dance public house
cankered to a cliff edge.
Whirlpool hearts frothing with jetsam.

      Hot little engines.
      Some rattle on blown valves:

Starched hearts folded like napkins.
Boned hearts folded like batwings.
Deadeye hearts. Bullseye hearts.
Peacock hearts, stuck with fat braided sequins.
Freeway hearts studded with cat's eyes.
Obelus hearts hanging by a thread.
Vivarium hearts, backlit, stuffed with iguanas.

      At night, they chitter like circuit-board,
      a riviere of gibbering binary.

Magpie as gambler

Here he comes, love this guy, chack–chacking
like a cue-ball off the break. It's the smart snickersnack
of the Scissorman, or a rattling stack of easy chips,
all bets, roulette, oh yes. Spick-and-span, pin-prick neat
with a livery fit for thief. He's a rascal, a two-bit punk
in a three-piece. A stitch-up artist, a silent era roll-me-over-
in-monochrome-Romeo. Tommy guns, dominoes,
uckers, boys! Jounced like knuckles, or Annabel's dice
gone cock-eyed, snake-eyed, would-I-wouldn't-I'd.

So what'll it be? A golden boy? A silver tongue,
a lugubrious Captain? A take-me-anywhere-anytime
Valentine? A knife in the ribs, something in scarlet?
The cruel one, the smart one, or one with a secret?
Shuffle and nudge, eyes on the cup, lady or tiger
or aces or duds. Where is he, that guy, that short-circuit
whipcrack, that out-and-out hustler, that joymonger-jack?
He's off. You're cleaned out. The deck is all jokers,
the joint's full of snakes and your pocket's been picked.

The Fossils in the Square and Compass

Oh yes –
in every chunk of rock   a prickly genie!
Some were dull: a spindly comb   some pasta quills   a dollhouse naan
and others better, better for being strange
                    and strange for being gut-familiar –
braided knuckles   curled umbilicals   a crazy-paving slab of fingernails
                        best of all
were those with faces, limbs, and all the rest,
propelled on toothpicks, mouth harps, bony paddles –
                        bonsai goblins – leering, sulking, puzzled.

We fitted and identikitted   violin-bow noses, pocky eyes,
the mute indignity of gogging mouths,
            the awkward poses. Said *fossil*
                till it made us laugh, and then
found every chance to say the word again   till we were roaring, shaking,
and *everything* was funny –
            the whole of Dorset rocked back on its heels,
                        bent double, heaved and cracked –
    The sallow friezes blanked us. Their moony cargo grinned and ogled back.

The long hot day parked up outside the pub –
the six of us marauding up the coast   to tyrannise the tea rooms, stick our fingers
        into cliffs and bric-à-brac and fish and chips –
                a cyclone fizzing in a china cup,
raucous   incandescent   breathless   sprung   on the thin hilarity of holiday
and being young
            with two hours still to go till drinking-up.

I have the photographs: we grin and grin
and so we might
when the bell will never ring, when our glasses
remain full, with betrayal
and other monsters tucked up tight
in the stony bluff of other people's lives.

40

And it's awkward
that these flat-packed ghosts survive:
a flickerbook and record of a joke
no longer funny.
        The years lay down in layers. Underneath,
we strike our stupid poses, bare our teeth.
We're stuck there now. Our smiles are hard like flint.

Follow the Lady

The three-way mirror split her three-card deck.

A.S. QUINTE, *The Vanity Mirror*

The first belongs to the world. Known by this argument
  of artifice and accident: gypsum, almond, opal, bone,
river pearl and dental gold.

                        The second

is mine alone. I'd know her anywhere
  by the precise syntactic script of cartilage
helixed at each ear; the proposition posed
  by the yoke of muscle – just visible now –
that meathooks jaw to collarbone.

                        The third

I cannot see. The complicit frame
  is a blind door, locked on an empty room. I never know
where she goes, or what she does. She frightens me.

52 Card Pickup

nec te quicquam nisi ludere oportet

Start small. One half-open eye may survey thirty
square feet of bed for several hours. Note that not one
of the seven shining hells you built is half as hot
as this field of white linen. Know all your dreams
are now the same six confidence tricks, shuffled.

Trust nobody. Not the old goon at the instruments:
the nerves splutter imperatives, but all news
is duff gen, scrambled, haywire. Be resigned,
if not accustomed, to the rank flue that opens
between heart and mouth. Learn to bluff, and bluff.

Get superstitious. Develop a taste for patterns, pairs,
but know that you're all out of luck. Here you are
sinking the black on a sure shot, snake-eyed, dropped
right in it with no getaway. You've got one bad hand
and you'll play it. Sweet nothing, and you've stuck.

Tally up. Find the same spilt deck, the same face
turning up, whichever way you look at it. Bluff,
but fool no one. There he is again, the duff joist
that brings the whole lot down. This is the house.
This is you, in bed at noon. Weeks pile up, discarded.

Love song for a Minotaur

You're lost, my love, you've lost your way,
I don't know how to find you now.
You tossed your head and went away,
the walls shot up and curved around –

a knot was tangled on the ground
and when you went, it slid and shut.
The walls shot up and curved around
I can't get in, you can't get out.

A knot was tangled on the ground,
a knot was tangled in your heart.
The road was long and looped around
and hooked its ending to its start.

The road was long and looped around,
a riddle ran around its rim,
it slid and shut without a sound,
it shut me out, and shut you in.

A riddle is a tricksy thing –
it hooks its ending to its start.
I don't know how to work the string
that rigged a bloodknot in your heart.

I don't know how to work the string,
I don't know how to break the knot,
the heart is such a tricksy thing,
it shuts you in, or shuts you out.

A knot was tangled in your heart,
it tightened, tightened, every day.
I skipped around and played my part
but nothing I could do or say

could keep the road from curving round,
or turn your head, or break the day.
There is a riddle in the heart
that murmurs *go* when you should stay –

it shows you things you're dreaming of,
it picks them up and puts them down.
The world is full of monsters, love,
I don't think I can save you now.

The road curves on and on and on
with no way in, and no way out.
I couldn't follow. Now you're gone,
and no one else can reach you now.

The Lesson from the Snake

And we might take a tip from you –
split-mouth, doubler, underling –
who can at all times entertain
two propositions on the tongue, two
crooked and opposing things.

She loves me and *she loves me not*
so says the double-talking snake.
Both are real but one is not
and both are true before you speak.

Tell her every vinegar thing   Don't tell. Gulp the acid down
you've swilled and swilled around the mouth.   and smile and smile and bite your tongue.
Spill the lot, spit it out.   *Keep it secret, keep it in.*
What happens then?   What happens then?
I couldn't say.   *I couldn't say.*

Forks and forks: tangential ways
divide in two and two again, two
pairs of doubles take a turn
on what they do and do not say.
And all are true before you speak
(*true and not true* says the snake).
Uncertain futures bifurcate
and every one belongs to you.

She loves me, and *she loves me not*
and both are true until you speak.
Better by far to hold your tongue
and both of them can't not be true.
Futures, futures says the snake –
in one she will belong to you.

Fetch

Who is this who is coming. And which one of us
is keeping watch. I watch your eye, that stichic jig
as it snags and snags and snags on blackout fields.
Copses, snickets, stiles. But what about the rector,
hunched in the dark, tap-tapping the wall of a well.
Oh, he can't take it back now. Not with that curse
on him like a collar. No, friend, that's not my coat.
And it's not the ugly thing in the alcove any more,
it's this hungry one who tugs and begs and whines
and says he's me. What happens when you whistle.

Arterial

I'm only half-surprised to find the heart
stranded half-way down the M4. This is not,
as you might think, a metaphor. The cats' eyes
all join up and there it is, red-raw and chugging.

The stereo's on the blink. So it's the racy roar
of eighty miles an hour in the dark, and that hot,
nagging tattoo – a doom-drum, counting down.
Three years ago I split the thing in two,

left one half of it in town, lobbed the other
out beyond the London Orbital. Now here it is,
jammed crudely back together, flashing red.
Just like my mother always said – *leave one man*

for another, and you leave the better part of you.
She knew a thing or two about the heart, its plush
interiors, dim-lit. The heart has four red rooms,
through which the blood is pushed in roughly rhythmic

stops and starts. Think of the poor dull traffic,
nudged from heart, to brain, to gut, and back again.
Once I read that the heart can only travel
at walking pace, so it can't keep up this shuttle,

shuttle, shuttle. *These are not helpful thoughts*,
said the therapist, behind her wedded fingers.
Also – *We cannot treat you for a broken heart.*
I went away with sertraline instead – a little oil

for a scrapped Tin Man. I'm counting down the junctions.
All the while, that little tyrant's in his palanquin,
drunk on his drumroll. You draw a broken heart
with a cartoon fracture line, like the house

built on a fault, walls gone, all rooms exposed.
You can die of a broken heart, something to do
with the vagus nerve, and enough rancid adrenalin.
At eighty miles an hour, I find it hard

not to think of myself as a rope-bag full of blood
thrown forward faster than it was meant to go –
the ventricles, the veins and valves, the arteries,
whose *A* is a rude mnemonic, and also means

away. Away we go, my tin can and my palanquin,
my unhelpful thoughts, my little scrawl of blood.
Anyway, I pulled off at Membury to write you this
while the wipers beat their soft, half-hearted thud.

All along, the ivy

Until you're known in my profession as a monster, you're not a star.
BETTE DAVIS

Sweet Charlotte.
You never noticed it, but now

sprawled helices, intricate, that lush intent
menace everything.
They will sell this house from under you.
                Supple, hush hush.
It plays patience, has nice manners.

        They will take you away.

            Stay still. It presses,
pinches, knows intimate details. It must,
it must insist.

           The ivy
is vigorously literal, has no feel for suspense.
It knew all along –

the gun and the blanks, the drugs in the supper,
Jewel and Jewel's secrets.

         Spirochetes, vertices,

the script and the script's whorls.
It winches, squeezes, keeps schtum.

Darling Jane –
you can't see it from the window,
but there it is, just out of shot –

the wall, the whole brick span of it,
prinked in skinny fists.
           Oh, it must insist

on the tussle, on the beach scene,
the vaudeville routine –
Joan Crawford's dead. Good.

It knew the lines before you did.

You know, Margo,
it's a funny business

    the things you drop on your way up the ladder

the things you forget.

What next, Bet?
The girl left waiting
in the vacant lot, who didn't look the part

    Oh, I thought I would die. Just thought I would die.

or mad dame, hooley,
sharp slut, boot-leather,
owl-eyes, rag-bag, bitch – *how*

completely you belong to me –

Smile for the camera. Let it curl at your ear.
It will remember you to her.

Key

Strung up like this, you've got me, boy,
I'm yours. Better dress those knots before
I count to ten. Lark's head, bowline, daisy-chain –

it's wicked fun, but it's a game. Ah, but now
you're scared again – the empty bed, the rifled
drawers, the busted hinges squawking *nevermore* –

Well sure, there's a life hung in the cupboard,
and it twitches when I twitch, the stitches pull.
But there's a hundred more beyond this room

and I'm still here. Listen now, it's really simple –
you've got something, and it belongs to me.
I don't mean that old skin, the useless key

you fret and fret about, wide-eyed and seal-slick.
The door was open all along. The knot's secure.

Spook and the Jewel Thief

It's a love song, goes like this –
the thief,
        the locks,
               the lasers,
smash and grab –
lightening, wowzers.
  Easy-peasy.

That's Annie. *Fingers* Annie.
Magpie Annie.
       What a girl –
             knows every trick,
got every skill –
all the lines, killer smile, smart as satchels,
that's our Annie. Lock-pick savvy.

And ah, she loves them all –
diamonds for the grim pizzazz,
that *rude*, unruly fission –

emeralds for audacity,
a sapphire like an asterisk –

Prickling little stars of hard precision –

      they jitterbug like urchins in her fist.

Sweet Annie.
Got names for all her lovelies –

Ginpit Nancy, Spectre, Ninker,

    Tesla, Gimlet, Rudy, Ohm.

Eyes like dinner-gongs for every lure,
for every spinner,
                    loves the lot.

Honey, rotgut, ginger,
that's our Annie.

*

That is –

till she meets chilly Mister Spook.

    What's this what's this

That stack of splints, that spider,
wind-wrecked deckchair,
Mister Spook.

Eyes like leaky ray-guns.
With his zither, with his rayon,
Mister Spook –

long and loomy as a taper.
Man, I'd like to meet his tailor.
So unhappy, singular,
a black-hole-in-an-alcove,

no friend of mine, no gentleman,
no good, that Mister Spook.

Ah. But Oh.
The slipknot sliding shut,
those icy tokens –
    clink clink clink
the zeroes stacking up, gut to gullet.
Scissored, skilletted. *I'm done for*. Boy oh boy –
It must be love.

Well, that's that.
Snapped taut like leather straps.
She's banjaxed, hobbled, hamstrung,
          on the rack for Mister Spook.

Oh, it's a dose all right —
It's freon down the marrow.
It's quartzy little jitters
like they've nicked her with a scalpel,
like the ice has gone beneath her,
like she's gone all out with zilch —

Alley-oop, and up-and-out,
slingshot, slung between trapezes,
Jesus, God.

          What's that, Annie?

Oh Mercy, Mercy me,
you know I'm done for.

And he thralls his skinny arms around her neck
                    and hangs on tight —

          A pillion. A spinnaker.
                    A 'chute rucked at her back.

*

But now she's feeling mean.
Feeling see-through, feeling squeaky,
feeling thin
          as half a wish.

Poor dear Annie.
Never thought she'd lose a finger,
never thought she'd miss a trick,

before before
before she set her eyes on Mister Spook.

And what about a lock that can't be picked?
And what about a hole that won't be stuffed
with all the rubies,
        all the emeralds,
                all the amethyst there is?

She's looking in his eyes,
he's looking out the window.

        Oh thievy, thievy man.

Pockets stuffed with diamonds,
eyes on the horizon,
        he's ransacked every purse and every drawer.
        Poor old Annie.
They crash like splintered sugar as he chews,
and he chews —

bring the popcorn, have a ogle,
roll up and see the showgirl,

her fingers slipped, she lost it,
she's been and gone and dropped it,

for The Man Who's Made of Nothing,
                Mister Spook.

Poor old Annie.

*

No, no, no —
Clever Annie.
Kept a secret in her satchel
Kept a little something back.
Good old Annie. Poker-savvy.

Her heart's a cluttered cabinet
her heart's a raucous loom
her heart's a loopy troika
and it shuttles to and fro.
Looks like this –

a wildcat,

a crystal,   a wee zero of her own.

Clever Annie.
Kept a canny little nothing of her own –

And she lines a box with velvet
and puts nothing in the box,
and leaves the box for Someone Sly
to come and try his luck.

*

And oh, he wants that nothing.

And he scrabbles at its edges,
and he scrabbles for a join –

Oh he wants it, oh he *wants* it,
oh he's *empty*, oh it *burns*.

And the breath comes out all flighty,
and the pleas come mewling out –

in huffs and gusts and will-o-wisps,
in prayers and gasps and sobs,
like oxygen, like magic scarves,
like genies whiffling from a spout –

and soon,
there's nothing left of Mister Spook.
Wheedles like a spent balloon, that Mister Spook.

*

Clever Annie,
kept a secret like a locket,
            Clever Annie –

got a skinny little trinket,
got a dancer for her gables,
got him hung on string and tenters,

Clever girl.

She sets him in her ring, and his eyes are leaky lasers.

A sinkhole-in-zirconium, that *pit*,
that Mister Spook.

            What's that, Annie?

Yes, some people.

Some people chew you down to sticks and straw
if you're not careful.

Some people have their fingers in the drawer before you know.

Same old story. Goes like this –
the hook,
        the line,
                the sinker,

flipped and filleted,
undone
        on half a chance

                beware beware

and take care who you dance with, when you dance.

(Don't they know it's) The End of the World?

This place is a shot fuse, hot, bitter,
defunct. A dud. No one told you
you could end up here, reels stalled,
needle snagging on a burred *frick*.

They're all in on it. The carousel
and the Big Wheel, the pier lights
cranking a stuck waltz and one blunt thought
doing the circuit: you asked for this,

you asked to go round again.
Here you are, then: spent, dead-ended
with two brown pennies to your name –
one for the bandits, the other for the ferryman.

The Negative

It is true that she does not appear in the photograph. But who, then, was holding the camera?

A.L. PRIME, *The Thirteenth General*

You lost her in Hong Kong.
Between sleeplessness and dawn, between
the shutter and the flash, or in
the sluice of bodies on the overpass –
            you turned, and she was gone.
The lights on Lockhart Road were gold and green
and red and black. OH WOW, they said,
LOOK HERE
and CHECK THIS OUT –
                you'll never get her back.

You had her when you walked the Dragon's Back.
Now check the photographs. Now check again –
you thought you'd pressed her here, that blue-black smudge –
        a guilty ghost, windblown and hurrying
towards the edge. You thought you'd pressed her,
blurred, within the frame
but she's slipped off again, the drop of albumen
that slides clean off,
                gets clean away,
and thins, and forms a skin.

You missed her when the tide came sneaking in.
Glass and heat-haze, smoke and banknotes,
                orchids, fraudsters, burning paper.
The city wasn't real. *Perhaps, perhaps*
you should've thought before you brought her here.
Now try and find one drop of salty water
in the harbour.
Now try and find one counter muddled in
with all the others.   Ten million eyes,
                and no one saw her go.

She split between the impulse and the blow.
See to it: nothing's missing. They're all here –
twelve hours in the day,
    twelve spokes within a wheel.
A rainbow scrolls its banner on the sky.
Twelve generals keep their watches, shrug their shoulders:
not one of them has seen her come this way.
They say they haven't heard of her,
        and you don't have a picture. *Silly boy* –
you never even told them she was here.

Pasodoble with Lizards

In every house, this room. The two of us,
the two of them, and two eyes looking, looking back
at two eyes looking – double locked. A hall of mirrors.

The frills go up. The zoetrope's gone gaga. Lickety-split,
they're off again – two whirring figures skipping house to house
and room to room, and sticking to the shadows. Off we go –

in the aesthetician's house, the upstairs room. The gilt mirror
and its gila monsters, slumped and coiled and polished.
We watch them from the bed. Sweat fogs the glass. They move

whenever we do. In the hothouse, the reptile rooms. The tanks
are stuffed with bodies, lazy like dumped flex, dozens of them,
looped and doubled. Violet, scarlet, gold and black. Reflected back –

the clapped-out manor house, the red-red room. Fungus, brass,
red drapes, the full-length mirror. There they are again – two figures,
fugitives, gone with the snick of the aperture. But it's all caught

on camera – how their shadows whisk their tails and dash for cover.
In the penthouse, the ballroom: two figures, wheeling, drunk,
that botched one-two. A cracked-up mirror, and two archaeopteryx,

confused and karking, snared. In the picturehouse, the panic room.
Someone fucked up: it's all over. The couple clutch each other,
know they're done for. Here they come, *ATOMIC MONSTERS!*

razing tower blocks and power lines, a clumsy little number.
What an awful bloody mess they've gone and made. You, boy,
in your hall of mirrors. And me – or my projection – gone

when someone flicks a switch. The two of us, the two of them,
caught up in our reflections. It's all done with two-way glass,
with smoke and mirrors. Anyway, we made these horrors

and they follow us, they move whenever we do, keeping time.
I'm tired, love. This dance has skinned me down to nothing much.
Quick quick, we've got to hurry, set off running. Off we go —

our fingernails *tick tick* upon the road. And we could run forever,
but we'll never shake them off, these hooligans, our lizard others.
They think they're us. We don't know any better.

Pepper's Ghost

The wall onto the past is very thin.
How effortless it is to slip away.
And if he says she's gone, perhaps she's gone.
The wall onto the past is very thin.

He says he never thinks of her – but when
an empty room can fill with her, the way
an empty sky fills up before the rain –
the wall onto the past is very thin.

One flimsy sheet of glass rigged up between
her life and yours. And every night she plays
in crackled blues and blacks upon its screen –
the wall onto the past is very thin.

He never really loved her anyway.
And when she comes, it's just to do the scene,
repeat a gesture, spin a tired phrase –
how effortless it is to slip away.

But there's a hidden room beside the one
you live in now. And when she went away,
he shut it up, and something else moved in.
And if he says she's gone, perhaps she's gone,
    but then again,

the wall onto the past is *very* thin.

The Amazing Geraldine

Put a penny in the slot for Geraldine,
Geraldine –
      light up like a whirligig
when someone says your name.
      Don't let them see the switcheroo,
don't let them see the strings,
your heart's a bankrupt fairground, Geraldine.

Geraldine, Geraldine,
cut-string puppet, mannequin,
flealess circus, broken hoop,
a cave-in in a girl-suit, Geraldine.

      So it goes, so it goes,
gotta face the punters sometime, I suppose.

Hide inside the peepshow, Geraldine,
Geraldine –
  Part the curtains! See the Lady!
Have the greasepaint at the ready –
they love it when you're lurid, Geraldine.

Captain Webb's a goner. Lives in water
day and night
    A LIVING DEATH!
          (that's 50 cents)
you know, he's just like you are, Geraldine.

Cut the cards and crystals, Geraldine,
Geraldine –
give them flimflam, give them fluff,
give them what they want to hear,
they go home happy when you palm them off –

      but oh, some days –
     some days the mornings border on obscene.

Two dozen gurning horses, round and round,
and up and down –
the tune is so familiar, Geraldine.
Your heart's a tired fanfare,
        and it stammers on repeat –

I'm fine, I'm feeling better, yes, I'm fine.

MAYDAY has been cancelled

I wish to communicate with you

I require assistance.
I am in distress and require immediate assistance.
My position is doubtful.
                              I am adrift.
I shall abandon my vessel
        unless you will remain by me, ready to assist.

Your distress signals are understood

Do you require assistance?
Do you require immediate assistance?
What assistance do you require?
I am proceeding to your assistance.
Assistance will come at time indicated.
Can you proceed without assistance?
I am unable to give assistance.
I cannot give the assistance required.
Assistance cannot be given to you.
I offered assistance but it was declined.
Do you require any further assistance?

The Courtesan Jigoku Dayū sees herself as a skeleton in the mirror of Hell

(after Tsukioka Yoshitoshi)

A dead body seems a thing apart from you.
So says my friend, who has a thing for skeletons,

but here's that bony maniac again, grinning
from the mirror. Slender key without a lock,

a speaking clock that will not speak.
Who brings me this assemblage of hairpins?

The spivs are an off-day from the Pit.
They're wearing their best bowlers, and peering

round the frame, all knuckles, knees and elbows.
They've come to listen in. They want to hear

the exit tune the soul plays when it's plucked
from living tissue. But I won't be obliging them today.

The body learns the leitmotif the mind
will not admit: the tick of stirring clavicles,

the blunt ensemble underneath the skin.
I like to think this no-face dreams a girl,

wishboned on the proposition struck
by our reciprocal regard. My dull companion only grins.

Turn the Blue Iris

(after Dario Argento)

Part the velvet drapes, and step within –
the curving path that marks the curling way
to the *Interiora*. Yes, the place is plush.
This species of disgust is villiform.
Run your hands along the painted lilacs,
pendent and convolvular. Like viscera,

like that which should stay hidden.
A vortex of desire and revulsion
that twists you *closer, closer* to the bedroom
and its camera obscura. That dark chamber
of the *khôra*, and the pinhole peeping in.
A mirror finishes the trick, throws your image

on a screen. Now something opens
like a flower, spreading outwards like a sin –
the puncture in the pillow. The pinprick
on the pad. That beady blot you couldn't hide
that darkened to a stain. You're –
what's that word? *Exposed* on celluloid.

Requiem Shark

(after Jacques-Ives Cousteau)

He is coming.   The great *longimanus*
Lord of the Long Hands
glittering   razoredged
                            expressionless   a slender silhouette
like a duke descending,
              as a virtuoso might use
every nuance between blue and black

His actions have no logic,   yet   an elongated silhouette
    his configuration is perfect

He knows this by instinct,
                    and can profit from it   a pale silhouette

I know that the circles
are growing inexorably smaller
There will be some secret
                            rendezvous

The shark's round eye   his wide
black eye   a forbidden spectacle   that flawless silhouette

Pelagic silence   sudden   superb
senseless   purity of the void

The nine lives you might have lived, were it not for the nine thin spells through your heart

(after Robert Aickman)

Your sisters flash like jewels, bright as needles.
They're threading languid reels in the ballroom.
Your heart is young and taut; your heart is strung
with sparkling futures. Put an eye up to each one.

Diamond

Sixteen and juiced beneath the discoball.
Your pulse, a worried minnow. Repeating
rigmarole of knife and nerve, plastic cups.
Nitrous in the engine. Night-edge. Ice in gin.

Opal

City-mist, plaster-dust. An attic-flat with moths
erupting from espaliers of cracks. Moonbeams
over moon-things: tooth enamel, silver spoons,
flakes of eggshell. Milk blurting into vodka.

Chrysolite

Acid coo of limelight, plundered gemstores,
shattered baubles. The evening leaking green
into the Bay. This whole town knows you're a riot.
You're a *hoot*. Barman – bring another gimlet.

Garnet

Argon, blackout, aluminium. Kickback thrill
of ethanol, and sooty prints on naked skin.
The cowslick when the wick ignites, saltpetre
for a purple flame. Your lizard-brain, its pilot light.

Topaz

Here's swabbing alcohol, diazepam, and nibs
or needles. Streaks of ink. Here's boredom,
languorous as bleach. The bad news breaking
through the skin in urgent, thixotropic script.

Emerald

Another scene in the casino: shellacked black
of limousine or baby-grand, and glassy dice
and candied fruit. Oblong baize that prints itself
ad infinitum. Lime and mint conspire in a collins.

Turquoise

The map shows one last exit. And you take it.
Knightlike jink from 4th to 5th. The sky is *cobalt,*
coolant, curaçao criss-crossed with vapour trails.
Brand new blueprint: bright-lined superflux of *now.*

Sardonyx

Blooddrop sun, and rust. Rasping teeth of the sierra.
Clever footwork in the graveyard, half in love.
Now Mr Calavera tilts a grinning glass of mezcal,
tips the wink. The maggot in the dregs: that's for you.

Carnelian

A slug of single malt, and you're match-flare, imp
and spark – a foxy twist of filament: pure mischief.
All the stars go pizzicato, and the city pulls a long
and lovely mewling from your low-slung violin.

Envoi

Now look again: the past is drab as deadwood.
We're rotting in the heap that was the ballroom.
The years are spent, and all your bitter sisters
shut your careless heart with rusting sutures.

Ravens

Page fifteen of the *Observer's Book*
where I first met him, crouching, crook
with a raffle of feathers and a deaddrop eye
and flintlock beak and a vagabond look.

Oh, and me a wee lamb with my bleat buttoned up.
Me a wee lamb, with my mittens and fleece
and my merry-go-stagger and my picturebook.
Me a white lamb.
              But for one snuck look

in the hedge, in the ditch,
where I shouldn't have looked.
One quick peek in the hollowed-out hill
where Black Crick sat with his bloodybones book.

Handsome fellow – one stuck note
that jigged like a bone
in his raggedy throat.
I plumped my heart. Said
            Sing, then, brute.
and he opened his craw
           and the lines wheeled out –

     There's a unpicked stitch in everything
     Where the light runs out, and the bird gets in.

He creaked and he cracked
when they slammed it shut
and my fingers sang, and the blood ran hot.
Too late for that. The trap was sprung –

I was stung too well, and the bird was out.
I was hooked. I was hung. I had one red song
and it jigged like a bone
             in my hollowed-out heart.

And upside down and overhead
hung Bad Caw Rex with his beak strapped shut.

Poe had one, and it wouldn't let up –
one red name till his mind snapped shut.
Odin had not-one-but-two
one flew forward
                              one flew back.
In fact, every man I thought was you
had a bird at his back
                              and a black one too.

Cry three times and the deal is struck.
Cry once more and you'll never come back.
Cross my heart and hope to die –

There's a man downstairs with a message for you
and a hessian sack, and a gambrel hook,
and a torn-out page from a picturebook
and a bird in the black of his swallowhole eye.

Olly olly oxen free

All right then. Let's out the entourage –
the fright mask I've been keeping in the attic,
the switcharound that happens someday soon
if I'm not careful. The Lizardman, who waltzed me
through a fit of jewels and juice; the Puppeteer,
the Plague Doctor, the Goon. The Sleek,
who likes to dandle me above the things I want
then auctions off the lot to someone else.
The girl with all the gerberas (yes *her* –
I've not forgotten her). The Imp who whispers
Sister isn't pleased. The Bitch, who'd go for you
as readily as she would me, the Jenny,
with her fingers in the till. The Bride,
who means to leave you at the altar,
faltering and foolish, while she's skirts-up,
halfway-gone to Córdoba. The Hangman,
with his gallows-sticks, who draws a fingerline
across his cheek, and tells me nothing, now,
will ever be the same, not with that *curse*
around my neck. And the one who never
trusted you, who purrs her syrup stuff at 4 a.m. –
how being here is leaking, leaking luck
from every cut and scrape I got in getting in.

We have a good rapport. I pay the bills,
obey the rules, and mostly, we just let each other be.
But all the while, I know they're waiting for

the pavement crack – that fracture in control.

Call it what you want. But it took seven years
to learn a lie is a broken mirror, that an error
may be flipped from heads to tails. Now I've one hundred
spells and tics and checks to keep you safe,
but – let's be clear – I didn't make the rules –

why don't you tell me, one more time, how
                        none of this is real.

They love that one. They find you very droll.

The Quilt

The quilt's a ragtag syzygy
of everything I've been or done,
a knotted spell in every seam,
the stuff that pricks and pulls. The quilt

began in '96. I scrapped
the blotch batiks and brocatelles
each backward-bending paisley hook
that tied me to my town. The quilt

came with me when I packed and left
– a bad patch, that – you'll see I've sewn
a worried blot of grey and black
to mark a bruisy year. The quilt

advances, in a shock campaign
through block-fluorescent souvenirs
of seedy clubs and bad psytrance
and peters out in blue. The quilt

came with me when I ditched the scene
and dressed myself as someone new
– or someone else, at any rate
and someone better, too – I felt

a charlatan in borrowed suits,
and flower prints, and pastel hues,
but things had turned respectable,
and so I stitched that in. The quilt

has tessellated all of it.
Arranged, like faithful paladins,
are half a dozen bits and scraps
from those who took a turn, then split –

the dapper one, the rugby fan,
the one who liked his gabardine,
the one who didn't want to be   *another patch in your fucking quilt*
but got there all the same. The quilt

is lined with all the bitter stuff
I couldn't swallow at the time –
the lemon–yellow calico
I never wore again. The guilt

snuck into every thread of it
and chafed all through the honeymoon.
I scissored out the heart of it
and stitched it, fixed it, final, here –

with every other bright mistake
I wear, like anyone.

Phantom

That shady fellow's at the keys again.
A man who hides his face behind a mask.
He's asking where you were tonight, Christine.
He says you should have met him at the dance.

A man who hides his face behind a mask.
That's what he said, Christine, that's what he said.
He says you should have met him at the dance.
They waltzed in white and red and white and red.

That's what he said, Christine, that's what he said.
Behind the mirror, steps go down to dark.
They waltzed in white and red and white and red.
Christine, you let the devil in the dance.

Behind the mirror, steps go down to dark.
Beneath your dancing feet are tortured men.
Christine, you let the devil in the dance.
A satin stain is spreading down the Seine.

Beneath your dancing feet are tortured men.
What did you do, Christine, what did you do?
A satin stain is spreading down the Seine.
Christine, I wouldn't dance if I were you.

What did you do, Christine, what did you do?
He's asking where you were tonight, Christine.
Christine, I wouldn't dance if I were you.
That shady fellow's at the keys again.

Into

It's something with the keys. Ramshackle crew
of russet, fawn and fox. So many notches cut.
So many two-bit skeletons. A door, clicking shut.

It's something with the locks. A closing door,
a turning key. And somewhere quite obscure,
something working, sliding shut. *Tick, tick, tick.*

It's something in the gut – a skeleton clock,
a turning cog. Something working, sliding shut.
A small thing, clicking this way, moving there,

and tallied with the keys. Your skeleton crew.
One for every time you bent or broke yourself
in two. The way that opens up. That way. Go.

Red-rooms

Your mother's darkroom, ruddy in the safelight,
our faces swimming up through phenidone – *Oh Abigail,*

your eyes are closed in this one. What a shame.
In black and white, I'm faceless as a domino.

But how to sleep tonight, in the bedroom next to yours,
with my death-mask dripping dry ten feet below?

I'm wired for the warning. Later on, I'll get the rubric –
there's always something nasty in the red-room.

Keys to bloody suite – here's Jane, gone mad-cat
in the mirror, and waiting all alone for Mr Reed.

Here's the hellbent special agent, and the psychopathic
spaceship, here's the recess with its pitch of holy dread.

And look, here comes the Prince, he's apoplectic –
some clown has crashed his masquerade. *Again.*

And somebody should warn him. But no one has the nerve –
because there's something really nasty in the red-room.

You never know a red-room till you're in one.
The mummer drops his mask, the mirror breaks,

the key compels the lock, and there they are,
his exes, dressed in lace. The man I loved the best –

one chamber out of four forgot to function.

                    I didn't get the ending

till I watched the setting sun
play its mayday up the white walls of my bedroom.

I went to see your mother. She got out all the photos,
and twenty years went down in dominoes –

Such a shame, what happened. Such a shame.
Now the Prince is striding through, from the violet

to the blue, and I've seen it all before,
but I never see the warning light come on.

And he's gone, by the time I reach the door.
And he's gone, and he's gone, and he's gone.

The Great Escape

We gave the others the slip,
     snuck out the back of the discotheque,

        the rain came down in filaments,
strung, electric.

               No, *wait*

no wait, it was the cinema –

Macdonald fluffed his last goodbye,
     that's when we made a break for it –

       floodlit, filmic,

rattling through the fire door
         and out into the street.

The cine reels rolled round
       tick   *tick*   *tick*   *tick*
but we were gone.

          No, no, hang on,

it was a wedding –

      my borrowed pearls, your father's suit,
the prim expanse of tablecloth.

The starchy conversations folding neatly one on one –
before they did the speeches
          we were off.

Every time's the same –

         Come on, come on

It's you and me   and down an alley
through a window   up a stair.

We ditch the chitter-chat, the script,
the cranked-up, wornout numbers,

          the mirrorball, the screens, the cutlery,
the dreary boxstep of propriety,

and exit on a broad, flat plain –

                    static, *click*. And play again.

Keeper

Here comes lean Jack, here comes bare-bone.

Here he comes: the enemy who knows the system,
mister slim who works the pins. The trinket jack

that beats the ace, the guest who wouldn't wait,
the lavish little curlicue that stands guard at the gate.

Scraps for the Goatman

'As to an imaginary cry,' said I, 'do but listen for a moment to the wind in this unnatural valley while we speak so low, and to the wild harp it makes of the telegraph wires.'

I *Line*

Tunnels and bridges, platforms and arches, the straight-
faced rumour of the old railway. A green seam through the capital
   or a frayed axon, chugging its news down the line.

This is oak country. The deliberate work of knotweed, underwritten
with the quick copper taste of the city –
                     stingers and tin cans, piss and alleycats.

II *Nerve*

Web and telegraph wire, the delicate nerves of the eye. Blown,
   bulb-dud. Your instruments are no good here.

III *Rive*

Slip through the fence
               Slow, sly
you'll remember the way.

You can smell a river
a mile away – that weird, dank tug
        woodpulp, wet stone, rot
that tilts your handlebars like a hazel switch.

You know how it goes.
There's this language, traced
   in sprockets and rusted links
           blood, rook, oak
  and you know how, here,

language grows strange,
drawn out of you
    in a thin brailled ribbon, a dot-dash-dot, a seam
of sticks and stones
                    Break my bones
or a length of road.

IV *Dig*

Soil, brick, unmending stocking of rootwork,
dirt and iron, old iron, and things with hasps.

Watchsprings, skeletons – wrens and mice,
that small shorthand, strutted and hammered.

Dig. It's a thrill in the fingers, quick and nervy,
an adrenalin-current. A stammer of dashes, dits.

V *Fork*

The syrinx of the wren,
lark's foot, adder's tongue,
these two legs, willing.

Switch channels. Find the current,
an eel finding the one
in five that leads back home.

VI *Switch*

                A switch, jigging in the hands. Antennae.

                         just on the edge of vision.
    As soon as the thought roots, he's there,
A column of smokestack brick, a tree
                where a tree shouldn't be.

      Yarrow and ribwort keep lily-white vigil.

VII *Slant*

Watch sideways-on. From the corner,
from the top and tail of the eye.

He's a skinny one, thin enough
to slip through a crack,
                          or up the slant stair

to the room you always *knew* was there.

VIII *Plant*

There are spent things in the long grass
        silver buckles, golden pears

and tuberous fears
take hold, get leggy, go sashaying out

No-Eye-Deer

          Eely Agnes

Dead Men's Fingers

                    Creeping Bent

You'll know him in the bulrushes –
Wobbling, longleggedy, clattering
Jack-of-the-Borderlands.

IX *Split*

Sideways-man, hallway-man, patron of halfway places,
slipways and spillways,
                          jennies and changelings,
hybrids and mongrels. Two-faced Jack-of-the-Doubles.

X *Gate*

Split down the sternum
into his two guards –
one will always lie to the other.

XI *Cross*

Roll out the bones.
Cross yourself,
heart and fingers.

He's a wiry one.
Sinew, seam and lines
for my lovely. Arrow

through a penknifed heart x

XII *Pare*

Darling, I've lost my way.
Now I can't ever come home.
Why did you go, why did you go,
Darling, I went to play.

Darling, I went to play,
and Darling, I went to dance,
I missed a step, I missed a step,
and the Goatman took me away.

Very small, this warm thing

Small, very small, this warm thing
in the white grasses.
And the big knife in the bright kitchen

where Mr Chop slams one slab hand
on the chrome countertop, roars
fit to bust a gut.

Kick, run, get low down.
Be inkblot. Go kicking and running
and don't, d–don't look back –

be nothing – a thumbprint
on a page corner. There is harm everywhere,
flat-black and ravening, corvid-class,

and the token bone on the blond beach
is humming your theme song –

you've run so long, you've run so long,
you don't know where you go when you go home.

Change, and keep on changing.
There are toads stationed in the long grass
and no picturebooks with your name in them.

Spook and the Sunset

It's a menace –
      a big, bawling red,
the hot *bang bang* of blood.

The lovers in the park are red
like love is red, when *LOVE*
is splashed in racy red.
      It's an itch,
an inkblot tease, a test
that – yes – he knows he's failed.

Spook, saddest monster.
Skinabalink, half-thing.

      It's wrinkled silk, pitched
high on stilted hopes.

      Tomorrow will be fine.

The Pocket Diminishing Glass

Then it really has *happened, after all...*

And look who's waiting, leaning on the pole:
greyer at the temples, and frayed around the trim,
but still your villain.   Still every bit the scoundrel
who called the tune   and led you down the hole.
The ribbons are all ravelled   and the spell
is wearing thin. I think you might have won –
it's hard to tell.

                    – How late it's getting –

Tell the sun
to fold his yellow blades   and hurry home.
The portmanteau   has packed itself away,
the circus   upped and left   without a word.
The court is still in session   but the dream
is nearly done.   What else is there to do
but clap your hands together   and   exclaim

You're nothing – nothing but a pack of cards.

NOTES

Emma, you're a gamer (9)
Lines 5 and 6 riff off lines in Jane Austen's novel.

Hare (10)
I've been advised that this is the correct way to catch a hare with your bare hands, but have never had the opportunity to test it.

The Lemures (12)
The word *lemur* derives from the Latin *lemures*, the restless spirits of the dead. Carl Linnaeus first made the association in his 1754 catalogue *Museum Regis Adolphi Friderici:* 'Lemures dixi hos, quod noctu imprimis obambulant, hominibus quodanmodo similes, & lento passu vagantur.'

J ♥ (13)
In poker, a pair of Jacks (JJ) is known as *fishhooks*.

The Man Who (14)
Line 6 riffs off a line spoken by Mary-Lou in *The Man Who Fell to Earth*.

The Wolf Man (19)
Lines 51 and 59 are lines spoken in the 1941 film of the same name, starring Lon Chaney Jr.

You Know Who (26)
The opening couplet riffs off lines spoken by Holmes in *The Adventure of the Blue Carbuncle*.

**† ** (27)
The dagger, also known as the obelisk. The asterisk's bad twin, with many fascinating (if arcane) uses. It appears in the Rite of Exorcism, denoting the points at which the exorcist should make the sign of the cross. In chess, it signifies a move resulting in a check. More commonly, it indicates death, extinction, or editorial ruthlessness. The suicide-king is the King of Hearts, so called because he appears to be driving a sword into his head.

Black Lagoon (35)
The epigraph is a line spoken in the 1954 film *Creature from the Black Lagoon*. Line 2 is taken from the film's trailer.

The phrase *lucus a non lucendo* refers to an etymological contradiction or other paradoxical derivation; literally, it is a dark grove (*lucus*) by not being light (*lucere*). Similarly, Brewer asserts that the word *black* derives from *blæc-an*, to bleach or whiten, though Chambers considers this a confused derivation.

The Stone Girls (36)

The phrase *dies through the mouth* is a literal translation of the Spanish *por la boca muere (el pez)*. In the game of Lotería, the bingo-call that accompanies El Pescado is *El que por la boca muere, aunque mudo fuere*. The lines at the base of the third section are taken from The Beatles' *Carry That Weight*.

52 Card Pickup (43)

The epigraph is taken from Ovid's *Remedia Amoris*.

Fetch (47)

The phrase *Quis est iste qui venit (Who is this who is coming)* is inscribed on the whistle in the M.R. James story *Oh Whistle, and I'll Come to You, My Lad*.

All along, the ivy (50)

Lines 28 and 37 are comments made by Bette Davis in interviews. Lines 32 and 41 are taken from the 1950 film *All About Eve*, starring Davis.

Spook and the Jewel Thief (53)

Line 41 is taken from Warren Zevon's *Werewolves of London*.

The Amazing Geraldine (65)

Line 21 is taken from a fairground poster advertising 'CAPT. WEBB, CHAMPION SWIMMER OF GREAT BRITAIN, Now Living in the Water Day and Night.' Captain Matthew Webb was the first person to swim the English Channel unaided, and later took part in a number of stunts like the one advertised. He died in 1883, attempting to swim the Whirlpool Rapids below Niagara Falls.

MAYDAY has been cancelled (67)

The two parts of the poem are collaged from the International Code of Signals, a system of codes devised for maritime communications. Alphanumeric codes designate messages relating to navigation and safety; these messages, together with their corresponding codes, may be found in *Pub.102 International Code of Signals for Visual, Sound and Radio Communications.* Signals are sent by flaghoist, signal lamp, flag semaphore, radiotelegraphy or radiotelephony.

The Courtesan Jigoku Dayū sees herself as a skeleton in the mirror of Hell (68)
Line 1 riffs off three lines of Ikkyū's *Gaikotsu (Skeletons).*

Turn the Blue Iris (69)
Line 8 riffs off Julia Kristeva's *un pôle d'appel et de repulsion* in *Pouvoirs de l'horreur.*

Requiem Shark (70)
The poem is collaged from the book *The Shark: Splendid Savage of the Sea* by Jacques-Ives Cousteau and Philippe Cousteau. Requiem sharks are sharks in the family *Carcharhinidae,* including the deadly oceanic whitetip (*Carcharhinus longimanus*).

Phantom (80)
Lines 14 and 17 riff off a line in the 1925 silent film *The Phantom of the Opera.*

Keeper (86)
The epigraph is taken from *Henry IV, Part 1.*

Scraps for the Goatman (87)
The epigraph is taken from Dickens' *The Signalman.*

The Pocket Diminishing Glass (93)
Lines 1 and 9 are taken from *Through the Looking Glass, and What Alice Found There* and *Alice's Adventures in Wonderland* respectively. Line 17 is a line spoken by Alice in *Wonderland,* though I've tweaked it a little.